MINECRAFT
Ultimate Minecraft Handbook

By Kwick Reeds

Table of Contents

A Brief Intermission

Hey guys, before we get too deep into this book, I wanted to give you a quick chance to pick up my other book as well. It is available for a low price of $2.99, reduced from $7.99. Check it out while this deal lasts!

Minecraft: The Ultimate Survival Handbook

Go to the following link, or click here:
http://www.amazon.com/dp/B0101A14DK/

Alright guys, let's get back to the book!

Introduction

Hey there, and welcome to *Minecraft: The Ultimate Handbook*, and thanks for purchasing! In this book, you will be introduced to many different advanced Minecraft techniques, tricks, and secrets that will help you to start playing like the very best players in no time at all.

There are several different major chapters in this book:

Getting Started: In the first (and most basic) chapter, which is intended mainly for beginners, you will learn the basics about Minecraft. This includes getting Minecraft set up for your system, learning about the basic game controls, and other similar information intended for beginners.

Minecraft Biomes: In this chapter, which is designed with beginners and intermediate players in mind, you will learn about biomes, which are the different types of environments that exist throughout the massive, and constantly changing, world of Minecraft.

Minecraft Mobs: In this chapter, you will learn about the different types of mobs that exist in Minecraft. There are several main categories of mobs in the game, and among each of these categories there are many individual species of mobs.

House Ideas: In this chapter, you will learn about some epic ideas that you can use to create an amazing base for your Minecraft character. Also, you will learn about some useful home-building techniques that will prevent you from wasting any time.

Mastering Combat: In this chapter, you will be introduced to lots of different combat basics that will allow you to quickly understand the combat system. Also, you will learn about some powerful combat techniques that will help you to kill anything that crosses your path.

Minecraft Secrets: In this chapter, you will learn about some useful Minecraft tips and techniques that you've probably never heard of, unless you are a very experienced player.

Alright, that's enough for an introduction guys. Let's begin!

CHAPTER I

Getting

Started

Chapter Contents

Getting the Game

Creating an Account

Game Basics

Chapter Summary

Chapter Trivia

Overview of Chapter

In the first (and most basic) chapter, which is intended mainly for beginners, you will learn the basics about Minecraft. This includes getting Minecraft set up for your system, learning about the basic game controls, and other similar information intended for beginners.

Getting the Game

Though it shouldn't be too difficult to install Minecraft and begin playing it, there are several things that you should keep in mind when you're first getting started to make sure that things go as smoothly as possible. If you are not a Minecraft beginner, it is recommended that you skip over this section.

Basic Minecraft Details

Cost:

$26.95 USD/ €19.95/£17.95

Size:

Minecraft does not take up much space on your computer, and you will generally only need 1 or 2 gigabytes (GB's) of space, depending on the number of texture packs, mods, and single-player saved worlds that you decide to have.

Systems:

Minecraft is available on Xbox 360, PS3, PS4, Xbox One, PC, Mac, Linux, iOS, Raspberry Pi, and Android. The only gaming devices where you *won't* find it are on Nintendo devices.

Creating An Account

Before you can begin playing Minecraft on your desktop or laptop, you need to create an account on Mojang's website. Follow the steps below to do this.

1. Go to https://minecraft.net/store/minecraft
2. You should arrive at a page like the one in the picture below. Enter your details into the page.

3. After submitting your information, you will receive a verification message from Minecraft to your email inbox. Find it, and click on the link that is provided within the email.
4. After verifying your email, you can now buy Minecraft. There are many different payment options available for you to choose from, including Visa, PayPal, and various other options.
5. After entering your payment information, the game will begin to download onto your computer. After it is finished installing, click on the file and Minecraft will open up. *Wahoooo* – you can start playing now!

Game Basics

Minecraft can seem to be quite simple after you've been playing for a while, but on your first few days you are bound to be at least a little bit confused by the massive world, the deadly mobs, and all of the other mysteries that the game has to offer. In fact, when you first begin the game you might feel as though you understand a lot after playing for a few days, but really, the more you play Minecraft, the more things you will discover, and the more you will realize that the game has *so* much cool stuff for players to do!

To make your learning curve easier, in this section you will be introduced to lots of different stuff that tends to leave Minecraft newbies feeling rather confused. And for those of you who have been playing the game for a while, it is your choice of whether or not to skip over this section entirely, or to read it in order to reinforce all of the fundamentals within your mind.

Minecraft Controls

Below are the default controls for Minecraft. Remember that they can be changed in the "Settings" menu of the game.

- Moving Mouse ~ Turns the character (and the camera view) in whichever direction you point.
- Left Click ~ Attack OR Destroy Block
- Right Click ~ Place Block OR Interact with an Object
- W ~ Move Forward
- A ~ Move Left
- S ~ Move Backwards
- D ~ Move Right
- Shift ~ Sneak
- Spacebar ~ Jump OR Float Up (in Water)
- E ~ Inventory
- Q ~ Drop an Item
- Ctrl ~ Sprint
- 1 – 9 ~ Selects desired item from hotbar slot
- F2 ~ Screenshot

What is Minecraft?

Since its original release back in May of 2009, Minecraft has continued on to become amazingly successful. Winning countless awards, being one of the top-played games across the world, and continuing to gross millions monthly even now, years after its original release, it's no surprise that most people have heard of it. But what is all of the fuss really about?

Minecraft is a unique game that combines cute, blocklike graphics with real-world scenarios, and of course, more unrealistic things such as zombies, undead skeletons, and teleporting men that don't like to be stared in the eyes (*cough* Endermen *cough*). It allows players to create massive structures, to attempt to survive in the deadly world, to build nearly anything, to go exploring across the endless world, to socialize with their friends, to build rollercoasters, to build traps, and so much more. Really, whether you're 5 years old or 50 years old, there's not much to *not* like about Minecraft!

There is no "purpose" to Minecraft. This doesn't mean that you shouldn't play it though – there will always be something fun for you to do. What it does mean though is that you won't be forced to do anything if you don't want to: if you want to spend time building epic buildings, then you can do just that, but if you want to hunt down deadly bosses instead, you can do that too!

At its core, Minecraft is a survival game with cute, pixelated graphics where players have the freedom to build, fight, and do whatever they wish.

Game Modes

In Minecraft, there are several different game modes that you should really understand before you start trying to do anything too amazing. They each have some key elements, and are suited for different types of players. If you're reading this book, there's a high chance that you've already been introduced to the game modes in Minecraft, but feel free to check below to gain a better understanding of which game mode might be best for you:

Survival Mode: Survival Mode is the most commonly played game mode in Minecraft, and if you're having a conversation with someone about Minecraft, there's a high possibility that they're talking about Survival Mode unless they've said otherwise. In Survival Mode, players must gather resources in order to build things, they have a hunger bar which slowly decreases over time unless they eat, they have a health bar which decreases if they are hurt, and they can be attacked by "aggressive" mobs, and by neutral mobs if they attack them first (mobs will be explained later). Players have an inventory, armor bar, and when they are submerged in water, an oxygen bar pops up. This version is a good starting point for beginners and intermediate players, to get them acquainted with the basics about the game.

Hardcore Mode: Hardcore Mode is a less commonly played game mode that is a variant of Survival Mode, which is designed for more experienced players. In this version, when you die, you do not have the ability to respawn and the world is deleted, and you are redirected to the title screen. Also, when playing in Hardcore mode you cannot change the game difficulty. This version is good for veterans and those who are looking for a challenge – but beware that your world will be deleted if you die while playing in Hardcore.

Creative Mode: Creative Mode is a pretty common game mode for more creative and artistic individuals. In Creative Mode, players have unlimited resources, and can destroy any block (including bedrock) instantly. Also, there are certain new items in Creative Mode, such as spawn eggs (which allow you to spawn mobs). In Creative Mode, players can fly, do not have armor, hunger, oxygen bars, or health. If you are trying to create an epic structure, or simply want to avoid being attacked by mobs, Creative Mode might be the best choice for you.

Adventure Mode: In Adventure Mode, which is designed mainly for multiplayer servers as a sort of combination between Creative Mode and Survival Mode. In this mode, you can explore the map, but you can't destroy certain blocks unless you have specific tools, making it a good option if you're trying to create, for example, an obstacle course without having the players simply mine through blocks, or if you're trying to show off something you've created without having someone "accidentally" set it all on fire.

Difficulty Levels

In Minecraft, there are various different levels of difficulty, which are suitable for players of different skill levels. If you're a newer player, you might want to opt for one of the easier difficulty levels, whereas if you're very experienced you might want to opt for one of the more difficult options in order to challenge yourself a bit.

Peaceful Difficulty: In Peaceful difficulty mode, aggressive mobs (which are also called hostile mobs) do not spawn on their own, and when players do spawn them using spawn eggs, they disappear almost instantaneously. It's possible to die in Peaceful difficulty mode, but only if it is received very quickly, since health regenerates quickly over time. The hunger bar does not go down in Peaceful mode, and if you switch from a different difficulty to Peaceful, hostile mobs will be removed from the world.

Easy Difficulty: In Easy difficulty mode, aggressive mobs do spawn on their own, and will attack players. However, they do not deal as much damage as they normally would on higher difficulty levels. If the hunger bar depletes all the way, and is allowed to cause the maximum amount of damage, players will have 10 full hearts of health left. This difficulty level is good for new players. Also, in Easy difficulty mode, when being chased by Creepers, they will stop their explosion and continue pursuing you if you move a short distance away from them.

Normal Difficulty: In Normal difficulty mode, aggressive mobs do spawn on their own and cause the normal amount of damage. If the hunger bar depletes all the way, and is allowed to cause the maximum amount of damage, players will have only 1 heart of health left.

Hard Difficulty: In Hard difficulty mode, aggressive mobs do spawn on their own, and they cause more damage than they do in Normal difficulty mode. If the hunger bar depletes all the way, it can kill the player entirely. Also, Creepers will only cancel their explosion if the player gets a considerable distance away from them, making them much more dangerous than they are in easier difficulties.

Hardcore Game Mode: Hardcore is not a difficulty level, but instead is a game mode, as we mentioned earlier. However, it is worth noting that when playing Hardcore game mode, the difficulty is automatically set to Hard, but when you die, you will not respawn. If you die while playing Hardcore alone, the world will be destroyed, and if you die while playing Hardcore on a multiplayer server, you will be banned from the server that you're playing on.

Day/Night Cycle

In Minecraft, there are several different cycles throughout the daily routine. The two main phases in the daily cycle are daytime and nighttime, but beyond this are dusk and dawn. Each phase of the daily cycle has key aspects that differentiates it from the other cycles. Overall, the full daily cycle lasts 20 real-life minutes.

Dawn

Considering that from a morning through night perspective, this is the first phase of the day, it only makes sense to talk about it first. Dawn is a short period of the daily cycle that comes after nighttime and before daytime, and the moon begins to set and the sun begins to rise. The world begins to brighten up, the sky surrounding the sun will begin to get a hazy red color, spiders will change to their non-aggressive modes, and skeletons and zombies will begin to burn. Dawn lasts 1.5 minutes (90 seconds).

Photo Creds: http://minecraft.gamepedia.com/File:Sunrise.png

Daytime

During the day, zombies, skeletons, and most other mobs that you have any reason to fear will either have burned or retreated into dark caves and underground areas. The sun creates the highest brightness level possible (in relation to other sources of light, such as torches, lava, etc.), and Endermen will become neutral, as will spiders (unless they are already attacking you). This is the best time to do outside activities such as collecting wood, exploring, farming, etc. Daytime lasts 10 minutes (600 seconds).

Photo Creds: http://www.planetminecraft.com/project/lighthouse-of-alexandria-with-download/

Dusk

During the dusk, the sky will begin to change from a bright blue to a hazy-purplish-orange as the sun begins to lower, only to be replaced by the moon. At this time, you can simply retreat to a bed (in a safe area, of course) to immediately skip through the night and start the next morning. Skeletons and zombies begin to spawn and emerge from caves, holes, and other dark areas where they've been hiding to avoid being burned. Dusk lasts 1.5 minutes (90 seconds).

Photo Creds: http://minecraft.gamepedia.com/File:Sunset_In_Jungle.png

Nighttime

During the nighttime, the sky will be dark, and the moon will be visible. Due to the low levels of light, aggressive mobs like skeletons and zombies will roam around the world freely during the night, and spiders will change from being neutral to being aggressive. This is the most dangerous part of the daily cycle, since mobs are abundant, it's more difficult to see where you are going, and it's quite easy to fall into deep holes if you're not paying much attention. Nighttime lasts 7 minutes (420 seconds), but can be skipped by laying down in a bed.

Photo Creds: http://www.photominecraft.com/minecraft-mobs-out-at-night-photo/

Mobs

In Minecraft, there are lots of entities that roam across the world, making the game far more interesting. Some are entirely harmless, like chickens, some will attack the player if the player attacks them first (during the day), like spiders, and some are just outright aggressive and will attack you even if you've done nothing, like skeletons.

These entities throughout Minecraft are called mobs. Basically, a mob is anything that is alive, other than the players themselves, of course. There are several different types of mobs in Minecraft.

Chapter Summary

• Minecraft is available on PS3, PS4, PS Vita, PC, Mac, Linux, iOS and Android smartphones, and many other gaming systems.

• Minecraft follows the typical movement system using the controls W, A, S, and D. To attempt to mine a block or attack something, use the left clicker on your mouse. To place a block or use an item, use the right clicker on your mouse.

• There is no purpose to Minecraft. Players can decide to do whatever they want, making the game a great choice for creative individuals.

• The different game modes are Survival, Adventure, Creative, and Hardcore.

• The different game difficulties are Peaceful, Easy, Normal, and Hard.

• The phases of the daytime cycle are dawn, daytime, dusk, and nighttime.

• Dawn lasts 1.5 minutes. Daytime lasts 10 minutes. Dusk lasts 1.5 minutes. Nighttime lasts 7 minutes.

• In Minecraft, mobs are the entities that roam around the world, and can be hostile towards the player, neutral, or entirely peaceful.

Chapter Trivia

Question #1: What is so difficult about the Hardcore game mode?

Question #2: What is a mob?

Question #3: How many phases are there in the daily cycle, and what are their names?

Question #4: How long does the daily cycle last?

Question #5: What is the purpose of Minecraft?

Answer #1: In the Hardcore game mode, if players die the game will end, and their current world will be destroyed. Though you can save your progress, if you die even once it will all disappear.

Answer #2: In Minecraft, a mob is an entity that is alive, moves around the map, but is not controlled by the character. Mobs can be aggressive, neutral, or peaceful.

Answer #3: There are four phases in the daily cycle, which are dawn, daytime, dusk, and nighttime.

Answer #4: The daily cycle lasts 20 minutes.

Answer #5: There is no overall purpose to Minecraft, which means that players are free to do whatever they wish within the massive world.

CHAPTER II

Minecraft

Biomes

Chapter Contents

Overview of Chapter

In this chapter, which is designed with beginners and intermediate players in mind, you will learn about biomes, which are the different types of environments that exist throughout the massive, and constantly changing, world of Minecraft.

What is a Biome?

In Minecraft, there are many different environments, and each of these environments has key elements – unique landscape aspects, heights, different types of mobs, sky colors, cool lighting effects, and many other different elements. In essence, a biome is simply any of the many different types of environments that exists in the world of Minecraft.

As you travel through the world, you are sure to encounter many of the environments. Some are much more dangerous than others, and having a basic understanding of all of them is very important if you hope to play the game most effectively.

Overview of Biomes

Below is a list of the major biomes:

- Plains

- Forest

- Jungle

- Swamp

- Roofed Forest

- Taiga

- Mega Taiga

- Mesa

- Ice Spike Plains

- Desert

- Savannah

- Ocean

- Deep Ocean

- Mushroom Islands

- Extreme Hills

- The Nether

- The End

Plains

This is the first biome that was created in Minecraft, which tends to be the most common starting area for most players. It consists of grasslands, which are flat for the most part, but may have craters, hills, and small mountains throughout them. This biome tends to have trees, flowers, and many farm animals throughout it.

Since many animals tend to spawn in the plains, and it is also quite easy to collect seeds for a farm, this biome is a good starting place for newbies.

Photo Creds: http://www.planetminecraft.com/blog/set-biome-position-mod-mineideas/

Forest

The forest biome in Minecraft typically consists of a collection of trees that are close together, blocking out lots of light from the outside environment. There are several subcategories in the overall forest biome, and they all have wood as an abundant resource.

The forest is a great place for building a tree house, and is also a good place to go when you are trying to collect wood.

Photo Creds: http://beefcraft.net/news/version_news/1.7_update.php

Jungle

In Minecraft, the jungle biome consists of areas with heavily forested landscapes. In jungle biomes, the trees tend to be higher than in other forest biomes, and they oftentimes have vines spanning between them.

Jungles are the only place where ocelots spawn naturally, and melons grow in jungles as well. The jungle is a unique landscape is a landscape that is suitable for tree houses as well, particularly since the trees in jungles tend to be so tall.

Photo Creds: http://www.pixelpapercraft.com/papercraft/4fb1261e420119530c00014a/jungle-background

Swamp

In Minecraft, swamp biomes tend to have bodies of water throughout them, with moderately sized trees with vines hanging between them. Slimes (a type of aggressive mob) can be found in swamps. Also, lily pads can be found in the water; this is the only place where they grow naturally.

Photo Creds: https://www.pigiron.org/productions/swamp

Roofed Forest

In Minecraft, roofed forest biomes can be quite dangerous. In roofed forests, the trees can be taller than in normal forests, and their leaves often cover up a large portion of the sky. In addition, in roofed forest biomes there are also huge mushrooms.

In roofed forest biomes, there tend to be many dark places for aggressive mobs to spawn, so if you intend to make your home in such an area, it's best to place torches all around it, since mobs can oftentimes survive even during the daytime, thanks to the shade provided from the trees.

Photo Creds: http://minecraft.wonderhowto.com/inspiration/minecraft-1-7-whats-new-biomes-fishing-0149028/

Taiga

In Minecraft, taiga biomes tend to have lots of trees, and the ground tends to be a bluish-grey color. In the taiga, there is oftentimes a light layer of snow, as well as ice. There are trees in taigas, and they will appear to have snow on them. Taigas are similar to tundras, except they have less snow and fewer trees. Water freezes in taigas.

Photo Creds: http://www.minecraftforum.net/forums/minecraft-discussion/discussion/164665-problems-with-terrain-generator

Mega Taiga

The name says it all… or not. In fact, mega taigas are not related much to taigas, except for through their names. Mega taigas tend to have many trees, ferns, and boulders covered in green foliage. The dirt in mega taigas looks slightly different from the dirt in other landscapes.

Photo Creds: http://journeyofbokou.com/2013/10/25/pixel-updates/

Mesa

In Minecraft, mesas are pretty unique-looking landscapes that are filled with clay and hardened clay, both of which can be dyed in order to be used for decorations. Mesa biomes are a bit rare, and have cacti, red sand, and many other unique attributes.

Photo Creds: http://www.minecraftforum.net/forums/minecraft-discussion/seeds/323829-1-7-2-mesa-bryce-seed

Ice Spike Plains

In Minecraft, the ice spike plains are a pretty rare biome, which are a variation of the tundra. There are "spikes" of packed ice throughout ice spike plains biomes, and there will usually be very few trees in these biomes.

Photo Creds: http://fr-minecraft.net/img/biomes/full/IcePlainsSpikes_08.jpg

Desert

In Minecraft, deserts are relatively barren landscapes that have little life throughout them, except for cacti (which admittedly, are very plentiful). There is lots of sand in the desert biomes, as is to be expected, as well as sandstone.

Photo Creds: http://static.planetminecraft.com/files/resource_media/screenshot/1130/Desert%20-%20Ex2_236100.jpg

Savannah

In Minecraft, the savannah biome has dry grass, it never rains, and there are oftentimes NPC villages. In these villages, there are sometimes horses.

Ocean

In Minecraft, the oceans are vast landscapes filled with, wait for it...

WATER!

Ocean biomes can get a bit boring, as there's usually not much to do, and it can be difficult to get back to land. Sometimes, there are islands in the middle of oceans, which can be a *terrible* starting place for your initial spawn, with little food. At the bottom of oceans, for those who are adventurous enough to make it deep enough, there is a layer of clay, gravel, and dirt.

Photo Creds: http://topminecraftworldseeds.com/wp-content/uploads/2013/02/Stronghold-Ocean-1024x582.jpg

Deep Ocean

Deep oceans are another version of oceans, except for that their bottoms are much further down than normal oceans. Just as with normal oceans, there's *lots* of water in deep ocean biomes.

Mushroom Islands

In Minecraft, mushroom islands are a rare biome, where the ground is made of a resource called Mycelium, rather than dirt. If you place dirt on a mushroom island, it will eventually turn into Mycelium.

In these biomes, instead of trees, there are mushrooms, or more specifically, *giant* mushrooms. Also, while most other biomes have mobs like skeletons and zombies roaming around, these have *Mooshrooms*.

Photo Creds:
http://vignette2.wikia.nocookie.net/minecraft/images/b/b7/MushroomBiome19pre.png/revision/latest?cb=2
0120112193801

Extreme Hills

In Minecraft, extreme hill biomes tend to have mountainous terrain that goes high into the skies – high enough, in fact, that if you were to jump from the top of many extreme hill biomes, you would fall to your death. Take a look at the image below to get an idea of what we mean.

Photo Creds: http://epicminecraftseeds.com/wp-content/uploads/2014/09/extreme-hill-backside.jpeg

The Nether

Unlike the other biomes, the Nether is actually an alternate dimension. For all of the biomes previously mentioned, you will still be in the Overworld, which is the normal area where players usually play the game. However, to reach the Nether dimension you can build a rectangular portal made out of obsidian, and then strike it using a flint and steel.

In the Nether, there is lots of lava (like water in the Overworld), the normal dirt found in the Overworld is replaced with a block called Netherrack, there is a resource called Soul Sand which causes players to walk *extremely* slowly, and Glowstone. Beds do not work in the Nether, and in fact will actually explode if you try to use them after placing them down.

There are many dangerous mobs in the Nether, including Blazes, Ghasts, Magma Cubes, Skeletons, Withers, Wither Skeletons, and Zombie Pigmen. In the Nether, if you happen to throw an egg, a chicken can be spawned.

Photo Creds: http://neurogadget.com/wp-content/uploads/2015/08/nether-fortress.jpg

The End

The End is an advanced biome, which just like the Nether, is not apart of the main dimension. In the End, there are lots of Endermen, and there is also the Ender Dragon, a powerful boss which is *very* difficult to defeat, especially for newer players. The regular dirt is replaced with End Stone.

After you actually get into the End, you can't get out until you defeat the Ender Dragon, enter the portal, and "finish the game".

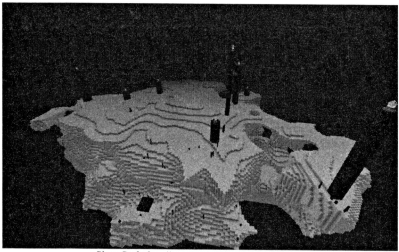

Photo Creds: http://vignette1.wikia.nocookie.net/divine-rpg/images/7/72/TheEnd.png/revision/latest?cb=20130129042559

Chapter Summary

• A biome is basically a Minecraft environment. Each biome has key elements such as the temperature, landscape type, elevation, and the mobs in the area.

• There are 17 main biomes in Minecraft, and many of these have subcategories, which fit underneath them.

• The first 15 biomes are contained in the Overworld, which is the starting location, which is safest for newer players. The Nether and the End are contained in alternate dimensions, which are much deadlier than the Overworld.

Chapter Trivia

Question #1: What is a biome?

Question #2: How many biomes are there?

Question #3: What are the alternate dimensions in Minecraft?

Answer #1: A biome is an environment in Minecraft, which has key elements such as temperature, landscape aspects, elevation, and the mobs that spawn there.

Answer #2: There are 17 biomes in Minecraft, but 2 of these aren't necessarily "biomes", but rather dimensions.

Answer #3: The three dimensions in Minecraft are the Overworld, the Nether, and the End. The Overworld is where you start, and the Nether and the End are much more advanced, dangerous environments.

CHAPTER III

Minecraft

Mobs

Chapter Contents

Overview of Chapter

In this chapter, you will learn about the different types of mobs that exist in Minecraft. There are several main categories of mobs in the game, and among each of these categories are many individual species of mobs.

What is a Mob?

Before we begin a chapter talking about mobs, it only makes sense to make sure that we fully understand what a mob is. According to the official Minecraft Wiki, *"mobs are living, moving game entities. The term "mob" is short for "mobile"."*

In other words, mobs are the entities throughout the world which move around, interact with the environment, and will sometimes attack the player.

Just like the player, mobs can be harmed by dangerous situations and objects, like lava, drowning, TNT, weapons, etc. In addition, they operate by normal physics (for the most part, that is *cough*Endermen*cough*), so will fall if you happen to, say, push them off a cliff "accidentally" into a big pit of lava, after being curious to see what cow + lava looks, and tastes like.

Unfortunately, lava-smoked cow ain't too tasty...

Trust me on this one.

Overview of Mobs

In Minecraft, there are several different types of mobs that you should know about:

1. Aggressive Mobs (also called Hostile Mobs) ~ These are the mobs that will present the biggest threat to you as a beginner. They come out to the normal surface at night (and sometimes during the day as well, if there's enough shade), and will attack your player if you come within a close enough range, even if you don't attack them first. Examples of aggressive mobs are skeletons, creepers, and zombies.

2. Neutral Mobs ~ Neutral mobs will only attack your player if they are attacked by your player first, or upset in some other way (such as by being looked at, in the case of Endermen). They aren't too much of a threat, unless you happen to accidentally anger them, or simply don't know what you're doing because you're a complete newbie. Examples of neutral mobs are Endermen, zombie pigmen, and spiders (during the daytime).

3. Passive Mobs ~ Passive mobs tend to roam around the world, minding their own business for the most part. They do not have the ability to attack the player, and will simply run away for a few moments if the player attacks them. Examples of passive mobs are chicken, squid, and villagers.

4. Tameable Mobs ~ Tameable mobs are those which can be tamed by the player, in order to be used for the player's benefit, mainly for the purpose of transportation. Examples of tameable mobs are horses and donkeys.

5. Utility Mobs ~ Utility mobs can be created by the player, and will follow the player around and assist them. They are very strong, and can also take quite a few hits. Examples of utility mobs are the iron golem and the snow golem.

6. Boss Mobs ~ Boss mobs are the most dangerous mobs throughout the world of Minecraft, and should never be hunted, except by experienced players who have armor, food, weapons, and potions ready. They are *extremely* strong, have tons of health, and are usually a bit difficult to find. Examples of boss mobs are the Ender Dragon and the Wither.

Common Aggressive Mobs

Creeper

Details:

- Will attempt to explode after getting within distance of the player
- Their explosion causes lots of damage to the player, and can also blast a hole into homes
- They have 10 hearts of health

Skeleton

Details:

- Shoot arrows at the player from within 8 blocks
  - They have 10 hearts of health

Zombie

Details:

- **They have 10 hearts of health**
- **They are very slow, and can only attack the player when very close**

Witch

Details:

- Witches throw potions at players to damage them
  - Witches are 85% resistant to magic damage
    - Defensively, witches will drink potions

Common Neutral Mobs

Enderman

Details:

- **They have 20 hearts of health**
- **They will attack the player if looked at anywhere other than the feet**
- **They can teleport, and can't be hit by arrows**

Spider

Details:

- They have 16 hearts of health
- They have the ability to climb walls
- They are aggressive to players during the night, but become neutral during the days

Zombie Pigman

Details:

- Zombie pigmen spawn in the Nether, and when lightning strikes within a 4-block radius from a pig
  - Zombie pigmen have 10 hearts of health

Common Passive Mobs

Cow

Details:

- They have 10 hearts of health
- Can produce milk by interacting with it while holding a bucket
- Drop leather and raw beef

Chicken

Details:

- They have 4 hearts of health
- They drop feather and raw chicken

Pig

Details:

- They have 10 hearts of health
  - They drop raw porkchops

Common Tameable Mobs

Horse

Details:

- Horses can be used as a very quick form of getting around
  - Some horses can jump up to 5 blocks high

Mule

Details:

- Mules can hold inventory items for the player
- Mules can carry chests to store extra items

Common Utility Mobs

Iron Golem

Details:

- They have 50 hearts of health
- They can't be hurt by falling or drowning

Common Boss Mobs

Ender Dragon

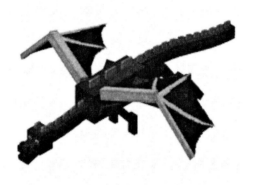

Details:

- **They have 100 hearts of health**
- **They will attempt to heal by using the ender crystals**

Wither

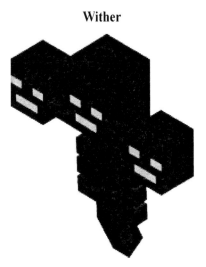

Details:

- They have 150 hearts of health
- The Wither is able to break most blocks that it touches, except bedrock, and various other blocks

Chapter Summary

- In Minecraft, a mob is simply an entity that can move throughout the world.
- The different categories of mobs are passive mobs, neutral mobs, hostile mobs, utility mobs, tameable mobs, and boss mobs.
- Passive mobs cannot attack the player.
- Neutral mobs can attack the player, but will only do so if triggered in some way.
- Hostile mobs will attack the player if they come close enough.
- Utility mobs usually attempt to protect villagers, but can be artificially created by players.
- Tameable mobs can be used for transportation, and for extra storage.
- Boss mobs are extremely tough, and should only be fought by experienced players.

Chapter Trivia

Question #1: What is a mob?

Question #2: Which mob has the most health?

Question #3: What boss can be found in the End?

Answer #1: A mob is an entity in Minecraft that can move around.

Answer #2: The Wither has the most health, with 150 hearts of health.

Answer #3: The Ender Dragon can be found in the End.

CHAPTER IV

Minecraft

House Ideas

Chapter Contents

Overview of Chapter

In this chapter, you will learn about some epic ideas that you can use to create an amazing base for your Minecraft character. Also, you will learn about some useful home-building techniques that will prevent you from wasting any time.

Why You Need a House

In Minecraft, having a home is one of the most important things that you can have to maximize your chances of survival, and to keep yourself occupied during the long nights.

Also, a home is an altogether necessary thing for you to have if you plan to simply go to sleep at nights in a bed (which allows you to immediately skip through the night to the next morning), so that you don't get killed by mobs in your sleep. And who wouldn't want to return to a beautiful home like this each night?

Photo Creds: http://justminecrafters.com/2014/04/27/epic-keralis-house-design-minecraft-pc/

Essential Elements of Your Home

Though everyone should have their chance to create some unique designs for their home, there are several key components that should be in *every* home. The things below will make your life (or rather, your *character's* life) much easier, will save you lots of time, and will provide countless other benefits as well:

1. Bed
2. Furnace
3. Chests
4. Crafting Table
5. Wall

Ideas For Your Home

There are several different key aspects that you need to pay attention to when you begin to build your home:

Size: How big does your home need to be? Are you going to use it only as a place to go at night to sleep, or do you intend to build a massive palace that's large enough for visitors to get lost in?

Location: Where is the best place to place your home? Near a lake, a pit of lava, a mine, in a tree, underground, on top of a hill – the answer to this question will definitely vary based on what you like to do in Minecraft.

Idea #1

Tree House

Photo Creds: http://www.minecraftforum.net/forums/minecraft-xbox-360-edition/mcx360-discussion/2010737-the-afro-tree

Idea #2

Basic House

Photo Creds: http://smallroom.co/simple-minecraft-house/classic-simple-minecraft-house-with-simple-house-3-simple-house-3-diamonds/

Idea #3

Basic House with Water Moat

Photo Creds: http://www.planetminecraft.com/project/a-house-with-a-moat/

Idea #4

Fortress with Lava Moat

Photo Creds: http://www.planetminecraft.com/project/small-castle-w-lava-moat/

Idea #5

Eye in the Sky

Photo Creds: http://www.minecraftforum.net/forums/mapping-and-modding/maps/1497757-242-

downloads-cloud-house-survival

Zombie-Proofing Your Home

It's great to have a nice-looking home that will impress your friends and make you feel proud of yourself. However, if your home doesn't keep you safe from zombies, creepers, and the other nasty mobs of the night, then it's as good as useless. There are several things that you need to do to "zombie-proof" your home:

1. **Add a wall:** Your first line of defense against the aggressive mobs of the night is your wall. If your home has no wall, then it's not really a "home" – have you ever seen a home in real life that didn't have a roof? Me neither. So add a wall, preferably made of cobblestone or something tougher, to keep yourself safe from the outside world.

2. **Add a secondary wall:** It's a good idea to add a secondary wall to your home, several blocks past the main wall, to ensure that you keep your home safe. Place torches on this wall, so that mobs can't spawn inside. This way, even if any mobs do get close to your home, they will only be able to stand outside the secondary wall, harmlessly – until the sun comes out and burns them to a crisp, that is…

3. **Add a moat:** It's a good idea to add a moat to your home, either in between the first wall and the secondary wall, or a bit beyond the secondary wall. The moat should be about 4 or 5 blocks deep, and at least 2 blocks wide, and you can fill it with lava or water. If you fill it with water, it's a good idea to add a drain-out area, which will drag deadly mobs to an area where they can't bother you.

4. **Place torches in dark areas:** If there are any dark areas near your home, you need to make sure that you place torches in these areas, to make sure that aggressive mobs can't spawn near those areas. Be sure that you have no dark spots in your home, or else mobs may spawn in your home during the night and kill you while you're in your bed.

5. **Build it in the sky:** Building your home in the sky, or at least a part of it, is a pretty effective way to keep mobs away from you. Also, if a mob *does* happen to spawn in your home that is 10 stories high, you can easily push it off the side, to its death.

6. **Traps:** You should learn how to add traps to your home so that you can make your home more resistant to the attacks of the mobs.

Chapter Summary

- A house is an essential part of keeping your character safe, is useful as a landmark for you to easily be able to tell where you are, and also is a great storage location.
- Your home should, at the very least, have a bed, furnace, chests, crafting table, and a wall.
- Tree houses, houses in the sky, and homes with moats are very effective.

Chapter Trivia

Question #1: What are some of the uses for a home?

Question #2: What are some effective ways to keep zombies out of your home?

Question #3: What is a moat, and what is it useful for?

Answer #1: A home is useful for many purposes, including as a storage unit, an area for your bed, a safeplace from aggressive mobs, and for many other purposes as well.

Answer #2: There are many different effective methods to keep zombies out of your home, including adding a wall, adding a secondary wall, adding a moat, placing traps near your home, and by placing torches around your home.

Answer #3: A moat is a trench that you place around your home, to prevent mobs from easily getting inside. Moats are most effective when filled with lava or water.

CHAPTER V

Mastering

Minecraft Combat

Chapter Contents

Overview of Chapter

In this chapter, you will be introduced to lots of different combat basics that will allow you to quickly understand the combat system. Also, you will learn about some powerful combat techniques that will help you to kill anything that crosses your path.

Basic Elements of Combat

Before you go throwing yourself into Minecraft battles and skirmishes with deadly mobs, and perhaps other players, it's important for you to understand how the combat system works. This way, you will never be outwitted by another player, and you will have the highest likelihood of doing well once the time for fighting arises.

Below are some of the main elements of combat that are important for you to understand:

- Health
- Death & respawning
- Armor & Armor Health

Health

In Minecraft, hearts, like the ones above, represents your health. Each player has 10 hearts of health, and can lose health in many different ways, such as by being burned, by being attacked by mobs, by drowning, by being hit by an explosion, by being smashed, and in many other ways as well. Your health automatically will begin to replenish if your hunger bar is at 90% (at least 9 filled hunger icons) or higher. Keeping an eye upon your health bar is very important if you hope to do well in battle.

Death & Respawning

When your character's health bar reaches zero hearts, you will die, and all of the items in the inventory will drop to the floor. However, they can be destroyed by explosions, lava, and even cacti (plural of cactus). Also, they can be carried downstream by water, if you happen to die while in the water. When you die, your items will fall to the floor, you will respawn either at your spawn point, and will have about 5 minutes to return to the location to retrieve your items.

Armor & Armor Health

In Minecraft, there are several different pieces of armor that players can wear to help protect themselves, and these are helmets, chestplates, leggings, and boots. Helmets protect the head, chestplates protect the chest, leggings protect the legs, and boots protect the feet. There are several different types of armor, which are leather, chain, iron, gold, and diamond – with leather providing the weakest level of protection and the weakest durability, and diamonds providing the most protection and being the most durable.

All armor has a certain amount of protection that it provides for the player, which is shown in the armor bar. This is a bar that comes up whenever the player wears armor, and the more armor icons that are shown in the bar, the more protection the player receives.

In addition, all armor has a level of durability. When players are attacked, their armor gradually gets weaker over time, and if the armor receives enough damage, it will be destroyed. Stronger armor (such as diamond or gold armor) has higher durability and will last longer.

Types of Weapons

Though there are many different types of weapons that can be used in Minecraft, there are only several different weapons that are purely designed to be used for combat. Tools such as pickaxes, axes, and shovels can be used for combat, but it's best to use weapons that are actually designed for combat, such as:

1. Sword
2. Bow & Arrow
3. Damage Potions

Swords are the main weapon that are commonly used in combat by most players. They are close-ranged weapons, and are quite durable.

Bow and arrows are long-ranged weapons which are less often used, but which are very effective for killing enemies for a distance.

Damage potions are used even less than bows, but can cause a nice amount of damage fairly quickly, but can be a bit time-consuming to find or create.

Potions

There are many different types of potions in Minecraft that can be used to assist players in battle, and to provide many other benefits as well. The main types of potions in Minecraft are:

- Fire Resistance
- Harming
- Instant Health
- Invisibility
- Leaping
- Night Vision
- Poison
- Regeneration
- Slowness
- Strength
- Swiftness
- Water Breathing
- Weakness

Chapter Summary

- To do well in Minecraft, you need to understand health, death & respawning, armor, armor durability, and several other key factors.
- The main weapons in Minecraft are swords, bow & arrows, and damage potions.
- There are many different types of potions in Minecraft, which are useful not only for combat, but for many other things as well.

Chapter Trivia

Question #1: How long do fallen items last after your character dies?

Question #2: What are the three main weapons in Minecraft?

Question #3: What resource makes armor the most durable, and what resource makes it the least durable?

Answer #1: After your character dies, the items that are left behind will last on the ground for 5 minutes.

Answer #2: The three main weapons in Minecraft are swords, bow and arrows, and damage potions.

Answer #3: Diamond makes armor the most durable, whereas making armor out of leather makes it the least durable.

CHAPTER VI

Minecraft Secrets

Chapter Contents

Minecraft Secrets

Chapter Summary

Chapter Trivia

Overview of Chapter

In this chapter, you will learn about some useful Minecraft tips and techniques that you've probably never heard of, unless you are a very experienced player.

1. Ice + Soul Sand = Extremely Slow

Walking on soul sand is the slowest thing in the magical world of Minecraft, right? Wrong.

By placing ice beneath soul sand, players traveling across it will move noticeably slower than walking across soul sand alone, and *much, much* slower than they would if they were walking normally. This can be useful for traps, trying to troll your friends, and for many other cool things.

2. Ice + Water = Extremely Fast

Placing water on top of ice allows you to travel along the water stream much more quickly than would normally be possible. So the next time you want to make a means for quick transportation, and don't have a railroad ready, then try to get ahold of some ice, and place it underneath the water to increase your speed immensely.

3. Leave a trail of torches when traveling underground

It is always best to leave a trail of torches (or signs) behind you when you're traveling deep underground mining, and even more so when you're traveling underground to explore a dungeon. Be sure to only leave torches in the area where you are coming from, and not to have torches going in multiple different directions, or you will get completely lost.

Also, torches can also be pretty useful when traveling far away from your home. Leaving a trail of torches will help you to easily be able to find your way back home, even during the nights.

4. Create a lava moat

Photo Creds: https://www.youtube.com/watch?v=jkGkkNQHc3Y

One of the most effective lines of defense that you can have for your shelter in Minecraft is a moat, and more specifically, a *lava* moat. For those of you who may not know, a moat is a trench that you dig around your base, that should be at least several blocks deep and several blocks wide, and should be filled with water or lava.

For obvious reasons, lava moats are much more effective than water moats. Firstly, they are extremely hot, and will kill anything that is unfortunate enough to fall inside within seconds – including your character, so be careful! Also, lava adds a natural lighting around your base, helping to keep mobs at bay.

5. Create a lava garbage can

Photo Creds: http://www.planetminecraft.com/project/lava-trash-disposal/

As we've all learned by now, lava is a very destructive force, both in the real world and in Minecraft. Powerful enough to kill mobs, melt ice, and maybe even dispose of items, perhaps?

Check, check, and check.

By making a small hole in the ground, filling it with lava, and surrounding it with blocks on all sides except the front (to make sure that you don't accidentally slip in), you will immediately have a quick manner to get rid of items that you no longer need. It's best to place this somewhere near your collection of chests, so that you can very quickly get rid of items whenever you feel the need to do so.

6. Do not use wood in your home

Photo Creds: https://everythingminecraftblog.wordpress.com/category/tips-tricks/

It is best to avoid using wood in your home whenever possible, since it can be lit on fire rather easily. If your home is made out of wooden planks or wood logs, a simple blaze that catches one of the wooden blocks alight will send the whole home up in flames.

However, if you are just obsessed with the idea of using wood in your home for whatever reason, then there is an option for you. Though wooden planks and logs catch fire easily, wooden slabs do *not*. So if you just feel the need to use wood, then simply use wooden slabs for your home instead of logs or wooden planks.

7. Use a system when searching for resources

When you're searching for rare resources such as gold, diamonds, or redstone, it is best to use a systematic approach instead of simply blundering away mindlessly, hoping that you'll get lucky and strike gold (literally!).

Gold, diamonds, and redstone all tend to be generated near the bottommost levels of the Minecraft world. It is a good idea to dig down (not in a straight vertical line – *not* safe!) until you reach bedrock, and to then move up several blocks. From there, mine a straight horizontal line about 20 – 40 blocks long. Go down the path, and branch out to the left and right every 2 to 3 blocks. In each "branch" mine about 5 blocks horizontally, and if you encounter any valuable resources, continue mining in that same area until you've collected them all. Then, move on to the next branch.

8. Stop water and lava with ease

Water, and lava – things that have brought the death of many careless Minecraft adventurers. In the best of situations, they can give you a nice scare as you see water rushing towards you as you sit innocently at the bottom of a dark hole, and at worst, you can sit roasting alive, as you suddenly fall into a pit of lava while mining. Yet with a couple of the right tactics, they can be tamed rather easily, by any Minecrafter.

So how can we go about taking control of water and lava? First of all, by placing pressure plates in the path of lava or water, you can immediately stop the water or lava from traveling any further. Also, by placing signs or ladders in the path of water or lava, you can stop them from flowing further.

9. Fight Endermen at their feet

When fighting Endermen (which might not be such a good idea for newer players), it is best to attack their feet. When you look at their upper legs, head, or torso they will get angry and attack you. But if you get close enough by looking at their feet, you can attack them. To ensure your safety, you can stand under a cluster of blocks that is 2 blocks high – since Endermen are 3 blocks tall, they would not be able to attack you – in other words, you'd be safe!

10. Milk gets rid of effects

If you've been poisoned, have recently eaten rotten meat, or simply want to remove the effects of a potion for whatever reason, simply take a gulp of milk. For some reason, milk removes any effects that are currently impacting your character. As such, they can be very useful for carrying around to get rid of poison, and other unwanted effects that might happen to impact your character.

11. Create landmarks

When you are traveling around the world in Minecraft, it is best to leave tall landmarks in the general direction that you're coming from, so that you can easily find your way back when the time comes. If possible, it's also a good idea to place a torch or two on the side of the landmark, so that you can easily see it, even during the nights.

Landmarks should be about 10 – 20 blocks higher than the rest of the landscape, so that you can easily find them. If possible, it's a good idea to use natural things that stand out like mountains, unusually large trees, and other similar objects as landmarks, and to simply place a few blocks on them so that you can immediately know that you came from that direction.

12. Upgrade your map

Tired of your basic map? Well in case you haven't figured it out by now, you can actually upgrade your map, once you've explored enough of the areas on the current map.

To upgrade your map, place it in the middle of your crafting table, and fill the eight other slots with paper. You will have the option to upgrade it, and you can upgrade it a maximum of four times. Upgrading your map gives it the ability to keep track of a far larger landscape.

13. Place torches to breathe in water

If, while drowning under water, you are adjacent to a block, you can place a torch on that block to be able to breathe for a moment. In this moment, your oxygen bar will reset, making it much more likely that your character will survive (or at the very least, make it a bit closer to the surface before drowning, if you're particularly unlucky).

14. Throw potions above you

Instead of throwing potions at the ground ahead of you, you should throw them into the air directly above you, to maximize the effects. When you throw them in front of you, though the effects are still quite powerful, they become much more powerful when you throw the potions above you.

Chapter Summary

1. Ice + Soul Sand = Extremely Slow
2. Ice + Water = Extremely Fast
3. Leave torches when going underground
4. Create a lava moat
5. Create a garbage can… with lava
6. Do not use wood in your home
7. Use a system when searching for gold, diamonds, or redstone
8. Stop water or lava
9. Fight Endermen at their feet
10. Milk gets rid of effects
11. Create landmarks
12. Upgrade your map
13. Place torches to breathe in water
14. Throw potions above you

Chapter Trivia

Question #1: What's the way to make people walk the slowest way possible in Minecraft?

Question #2: What's the way to make people walk the fastest way possible in Minecraft?

Question #3: What is an easy way to quickly dispose of trash?

Question #4: How can you immediately get rid of poison and other unwanted effects?

Answer #1: The slowest way for players to move in Minecraft is when walking on soul sand, with ice underneath it.

Answer #2: Placing water on top of water allows players to travel along the water very quickly.

Answer #3: By placing a small hole in the ground, and filling it with lava, you can quickly get rid of items by throwing them into the lava flow.

Answer #4: By drinking milk, you can immediately remove any ongoing effects.

A Brief Intermission

Hey guys, before we close off this book, I wanted to give you a quick chance to pick up my other book as well. It is available for a low price of $2.99, with a normal Print price of $7.99. Check it out while this deal lasts!

Minecraft: The Ultimate Survival Handbook

Go to the following link, or click here:
http://www.amazon.com/dp/B0101A14DK/

Alright guys, let's finish up this book!

Appendix

Useful links for you to continue learning:

- http://minecraft.gamepedia.com/Minecraft_Wiki Minecraft's official Wiki page, where there is information on a wide array of Minecraft topics.
- http://www.minecraftcrafting.info A detailed website that provides information about the crafting recipes for many different Minecraft items.
- http://www.minecraft101.net/redstone/redstone-basics.html A very useful webpage that provides information about how to use redstone in Minecraft.
- http://minecrafthousedesign.com This webpage has TONS of interesting Minecraft house designs for you to try out.

Conclusion

As is to be expected for a game as large as Minecraft, there is lots more for you to learn. This book was designed to get you started in the right direction, and to help you understand all of the most important concepts about the game. However, you will never truly become an expert until you get back to the game and spend some time getting acquainted with all of the different cool things that the game has to offer. So thanks again for reading, and good luck with your Minecraft adventures!